MW01102155

REMARKABLE
PEOPLE

Mark
Zuckerberg

by Steve Goldsworthy

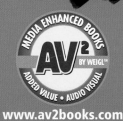

MEDIA ENHANCED BOOKS
AV²
BY WEIGL™
ADDED VALUE • AUDIO VISUAL

www.av2books.com

AV² provides enriched content that supplements and complements this book. Weigl's AV² books strive to create inspired learning and engage young minds in a total learning experience.

Your AV² Media Enhanced books come alive with...

Audio
Listen to sections of the book read aloud.

Key Words
Study vocabulary, and complete a matching word activity.

Go to **www.av2books.com,** and enter this book's unique code.

Video
Watch informative video clips.

Quizzes
Test your knowledge.

BOOK CODE

N 7 6 2 7 3 5

Embedded Weblinks
Gain additional information for research.

Slide Show
View images and captions, and prepare a presentation.

AV² by Weigl brings you media enhanced books that support active learning.

Try This!
Complete activities and hands-on experiments.

... and much, much more!

Published by AV² by Weigl
350 5th Avenue, 59th Floor
New York, NY 10118

www.av2books.com   www.weigl.com

Library of Congress Cataloging-in-Publication Data

Goldsworthy, Steve.
  Mark Zuckerberg / by Steve Goldsworthy.
    p. cm. -- (Remarkable people)
  Includes index.
  ISBN 978-1-61913-872-8 (hardcover : alk. paper) -- ISBN 978-1-61913-873-5 (softcover : alk. paper)
  1. Zuckerberg, Mark, 1984- 2. Facebook (Firm)--Juvenile literature. 3. Facebook (Electronic resource)--Juvenile literature. 4. Webmasters--United States--Biography--Juvenile literature.
  5. Businesspeople--United States--Biography--Juvenile literature. 6. Online social networks--Juvenile literature. I. Title.
  HM743.F33G65 2013
  006.7092--dc23
  [B]
                                2012018278

Printed in the United States of America in North Mankato, Minnesota
1 2 3 4 5 6 7 8 9 0 16 15 14 13 12

WEP170512
062012

Senior Editor: Heather Kissock
Art Director: Terry Paulhus

Photograph Credits
Weigl acknowledges Getty Images as the primary image supplier for this title. Every reasonable effort has been made to trace ownership and to obtain permission to reprint copyright material. The publishers would be pleased to have any errors or omissions brought to their attention so that they may be corrected in subsequent printings.

Contents

Who Is Mark Zuckerberg?

Mark Zuckerberg is the co-founder of Facebook, the most successful social network on the internet. A social network is a website for people to connect, communicate, and share ideas and interests. Mark created Facebook when he was a teenager. At the time, he had no idea how important it would become. Today, people use Facebook to stay in touch with family and friends far away. Companies use Facebook to promote their services and products to other people.

> *"When you give everyone a voice and give people power, the system usually ends up in a really good place. So, what we view our role as is giving people that power."*

Mark has always wanted to help people communicate with one another. Since he was very young, he has created new and different ways for people to stay connected. Now, he loves to inspire other young people to create new ways to communicate. Mark sees an exciting future for the internet. He hopes that younger generations will use websites like Facebook to make their world a better place.

Growing Up

ark Elliot Zuckerberg was born May 14, 1984, in Dobbs Ferry, New York and spent most of his early years in the small village. Mark worked hard at his studies in school. His favorite subjects included history, literature, art, and languages. He also did very well in astronomy, math, and **physics**. Mark's parents felt it was important to have many interests. Mark's father, Edward, introduced Mark to computers at an early age. His dad taught Mark how to write computer **programs** before he was 10 years old.

Mark liked playing computer games, but he also liked creating them. His favorite programs involved communication tools. When he was a teenager, he developed a program he called "ZuckNet." This program helped his father with his dentistry practice. It allowed his father's home computer to communicate with the computer at his office. It also allowed the Zuckerberg family to send messages to one another on their own computers.

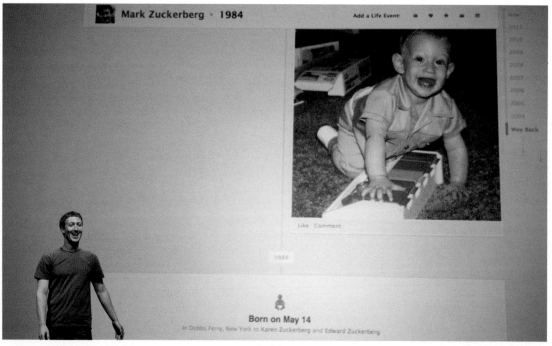

■ At a 2011 conference, Mark shared his baby picture to show how Facebook can be used to share photographs, music, movies, and TV shows.

Get to Know New York

ANIMAL
Beaver

TREE
Sugar Maple

BIRD
Bluebird

The capital of New York is Albany. The state's largest city is New York City. New York City is the largest city in the United States, with more than 8.1 million people.

New York was the first state to require license plates on automobiles.

New York's Statue of Liberty, a gift from France, was packed in 214 wooden crates and shipped to the United States in 1885.

IBM, a leading technology firm, has its headquarters in Armonk.

Think about it!

Mark Zuckerberg developed the idea of Facebook as a way to do something he loved and to help others. Think about what you really love to do. Is it writing, art, or math? Is it connecting with people or making things work? Now, how do you think these things might help others? Can you think of ways to use your talents to make life more interesting or easier for your family, friends, or the world?

Practice Makes Perfect

Mark spent most of his youth working with computers. He liked to develop computer programs based on the interests of the people around him. One of his first projects involved music. In high school, he created a music player called Synapse Media Player. The program could "learn" the type of music a listener liked and recommend other songs.

After high school, Mark entered classes at Harvard University. He studied **psychology** and computer science. He was interested in how people think and how computers work. He also recognized the power of the internet to connect people. In his first year at Harvard, Mark developed a program called Course Match. It helped students choose their classes. Through the internet, they could see what other students with similar tastes had chosen. They could also form study groups online.

■ Mark returned to Harvard University in the fall of 2011 to visit and speak with the school's computer science students.

Next, Mark developed a program he called Facemash. Users could view images of two students at a time, and compare them. The program was so popular that it overwhelmed the university's internet service, causing a major network crash.

Mark continued to develop more ideas. He listened to what his classmates wanted on the internet. These conversations led Mark to realize that students wanted a website where they could meet other students, share ideas, and study together. They wanted an online community where they could post photos of themselves and their own experiences. Mark saw the potential for a really big idea. That big idea would become Facebook.

■ Although Facebook was initially limited to Harvard students, it is now a worldwide phenomenon.

Key Events

Mark continued to experiment with creating an online community for students at Harvard. For an art history course, he **uploaded** 500 pictures to a website similar to Facemash. He asked students to comment on the pictures. This was Mark's first attempt to get people to share ideas with one another. The success of this site led him to combine it with a photo directory. Most universities had a directory where students could post a picture of themselves. It was an important way for students to make new friends. Mark developed a site that combined the photo directory with the ability to add comments. Facebook was launched from Mark's Harvard **dormitory** on February 4, 2004.

Next, Mark decided to link his Harvard site to the sites at other universities. He asked his roommate Dustin Moskovitz to help. Over time, the site was linked to universities such as Stanford, New York University, Cornell, and Yale. The connections then grew to several other schools.

Soon, large companies wanted to advertise on the site. Many companies even offered to buy Facebook. Mark decided not to sell the site. He wanted to keep it free and open. In 2005, Facebook began expanding to universities around the world. Then, employees at big companies began joining. By the summer of 2008, there were more than 100 million people logging on to Facebook.

■ While Facebook's international headquarters is located in Ireland, the company's base is found in Palo Alto, California.

Thoughts from Mark

Mark is grateful for a chance to connect people. He is pleased that he can offer the world a place to discuss ideas and make changes for the better. He shares some of his ideas here.

Mark explains his vision for social media.

"The thing I really care about is the mission, making the world open."

Mark talks about one of the most important principles of Facebook.

"For me and my colleagues, the most important thing is that we create an open information flow for people."

Mark talks about the power that social media can have.

"Creating channels between people who want to work together toward change has always been one of the ways that social movements push the world forward and make it better."

Mark talks about the power of sharing information.

"By giving people the power to share, we're making the world more transparent."

Mark offers thoughts on the future of Facebook.

"We are working hard to build a service that everyone, everywhere can use, whether they are a person, a company, a president, or an organization working for change."

Mark comments on the role Facebook plays in people's lives.

"The question isn't, 'What do we want to know about people?' It's, 'What do people want to tell about themselves?'"

What Is an Internet Entrepreneur?

The internet was developed to give computers a way of communicating with one another. This allowed people to communicate in new ways. Internet **entrepreneurs** like Mark Zuckerberg have seen the potential the internet has to offer. They understand that the internet has endless possibilities in areas of communication and business. Internet entrepreneurs are always listening to their customers and thinking of new ways to use the internet.

Most internet entrepreneurs come from the world of computers. They have backgrounds in sciences such as electronics, chemistry, physics, or **engineering**. They may, like Mark, also have taken studies in human behavior.

Internet entrepreneurs must have a strong business sense. Their main goal is to find ways to make money with the internet. Many website owners charge businesses to advertise on their site. Website owners can then take the money they receive and **reinvest** it, or put it back into developing their website. This improves the services offered to their website users.

■ More than one third of Earth's population, or 2.1 billion people, uses the internet.

Internet Entrepreneurs 101

Chris DeWolfe (1966–)

U.S. entrepreneur Chris DeWolfe is one of the creators of the social network Myspace. Myspace was started in 2003, a year before Facebook. Chris had a strong business background and knew much about **marketing** and customer service. When it first started, Myspace was the most popular social website available. Chris made Myspace unique with its focus on music. Users could upload their own songs and get new listeners to buy their albums. Myspace was the most visited website in the U.S. from 2005 to 2008, when it was overtaken by Facebook.

Sergey Brin (1973–)

Sergey Brin is a computer scientist and co-founder of Google. He came to the United States from Russia at age 6. At school, he studied math and computers. He was working on a **doctorate** in computer science at Stanford University when he met Larry Page. Together, they built a **search engine** that would become Google. The two men launched Google Inc. in 1998, working from a rented garage. Today, Google is one of the most successful companies in the world. Sergey's personal wealth is estimated at $18.7 billion.

Jeff Bezos (1964–)

Jeff Bezos is the founder of amazon.com, an online **retailer**. Jeff had a passion for science from an early age. He tinkered around in his parents' garage, making electrical alarms and conducting science experiments. He then studied electrical engineering and computer science in university. Jeff created amazon.com in 1994. Today, amazon.com is one of the most successful online shopping websites in the world.

Arianna Huffington (1950–)

Arianna Huffington is a U.S. writer and columnist. She is also the founder of the news website *The Huffington Post*. This website is one of the most visited and well respected sites for news and information. Originally from Greece, Arianna wrote many books and magazine articles while living in England. In 2005, she created *The Huffington Post* as a site to "blog," or write about important issues. Many celebrities and politicians, as well as journalists, now contribute to the site. Today, *The Huffington Post* is ranked one of the most powerful blog sites in the world.

Social Media

Social media is the use of websites to connect with others. Social media has changed the way individuals and companies work and interact with each other. Examples include Facebook, Myspace, and Twitter. They also can include social games such as Farmville or sites that allow people to contribute information, such as Wikipedia or Youtube. These forms of social media often include an opportunity for people to comment and connect with other users.

Influences

One of Mark's greatest influences was his father. When Edward Zuckerberg saw that his son was interested in computers at an early age, he hired a computer expert to teach Mark more about them. Mark's private teacher was **software developer** David Newman. David has said that it was tough to stay ahead of Mark.

Mark also drew inspiration from his friends. His friends would come up with ideas for computer games. They would draw pictures or write stories. Then, Mark would create a game around these ideas. Many of his friends helped him with the design of the Facebook website. People in the computer world and the business world also offered Mark advice. Apple Inc. founder Steve Jobs helped Mark organize his company to run smoothly.

■ Before he died in 2011, Steve Jobs advised Mark on how to sharpen his company's focus and how to build a good management team for Facebook.

Mark also finds inspiration from the users of Facebook. He listens to their wants and needs and works to make the site better. He even asks users to come up with their own solutions. If he likes a person's idea, he will sometimes offer the person a job with the company.

MARK'S FAMILY

Mark's mother, Karen, is a psychiatrist. His father, Edward, is a dentist. Mark also has three sisters, Randi, Donna, and Arielle. The family is close. Even though they now live apart from each other, the family often gets together for vacations and visits. At one time, Randi even worked for Mark at Facebook.

■ On May 19, 2012, Mark married his long-time girlfriend, Priscilla Chan, at their home in California.

Overcoming Obstacles

Mark had help from many people when he developed Facebook. Some people, however, felt their ideas were stolen by Mark. Twin brothers Cameron and Tyler Winklevoss wanted to build a social network and asked Mark for help. Mark developed Facebook instead. He paid the twins $20 million for the role they had in Facebook's development.

■ While at Harvard University, the Winklevoss twins, along with another student, created the plan for a social media site called ConnectU. It had many of the features that eventually appeared in Facebook.

Eduardo Saverin was another Harvard student who helped Mark create Facebook. He took Mark to court to get what he thought was his fair share of the Facebook company. Eduardo and Mark eventually came to an agreement outside of court.

Mark felt that living and working in New York State was a big challenge. The center of computers and technology in the United States has always been in California's "Silicon Valley." This is an area in and around San Jose. Many technology companies, including Apple Inc. and Google, have headquarters there. Mark knew he had to be close to these companies and their technology. In 2004, he relocated to the city of Palo Alto, California. This move to Silicon Valley helped make Facebook more successful than ever.

■ Silicon Valley is considered the center of innovation and development in the United States' high-tech industry.

Achievements and Successes

Mark has enjoyed much success throughout his life. He studied hard in school and earned excellent grades. Still, he was always pushing himself to do more. While in high school, Mark created a music player program. It was so well received that Microsoft offered Mark a job. Mark chose to go to university instead.

Mark has received many awards for his entrepreneurial skills. *MIT Technology Review* magazine named Mark one of the world's top **innovators** under 35 years of age. In 2010, Mark was awarded *Time Magazine's* Person of the Year. That same year, *Vanity Fair* magazine named Mark number one on its list of the Top 100 most influential people of the Information Age.

■ *Time Magazine* releases its Person of the Year issue at the end of every year. Mark was selected for the impact that Facebook has had on the exchange of information and for changing the way people communicate with one another.

Mark believes the popularity of Facebook is his greatest achievement. The website is ranked as the most used social network in the world. As a result, Facebook has brought Mark tremendous financial success. In 2008, Mark became the world's youngest **billionaire**. As of March 2012, his net worth was estimated at $17.5 billion.

HELPING OTHERS

Many internet entrepreneurs recognize the importance of giving back to the community. In 2010, Mark created Startup: Education. The goal of the foundation is to improve educational opportunities for children across the country. The foundation's first act was to donate $100 million to Newark Public Schools in New Jersey.

Later that year, Mark signed a promise called the "Giving Pledge." In the pledge, Mark agreed to donate at least half his wealth to charity over time. Others that signed the pledge included Microsoft's Bill Gates, billionaire Warren Buffet, and *Star Wars* creator George Lucas.

Write a Biography

A person's life story can be the subject of a book. This kind of book is called a biography. Biographies describe the lives of remarkable people, such as those who have achieved great success or have done important things to help others. These people may be alive today, or they may have lived many years ago. Reading a biography can help you learn more about a remarkable person.

At school, you might be asked to write a biography. First, decide who you want to write about. You can choose an internet entrepreneur, such as Mark Zuckerberg, or any other person. Then, find out if your library has any books about this person. Learn as much as you can about him or her. Write down the key events in this person's life. What was this person's childhood like? What has he or she accomplished? What are his or her goals? What makes this person special or unusual?

A concept web is a useful research tool. Read the questions in the following concept web. Answer the questions in your notebook. Your answers will help you write a biography.

Mark Zuckerberg

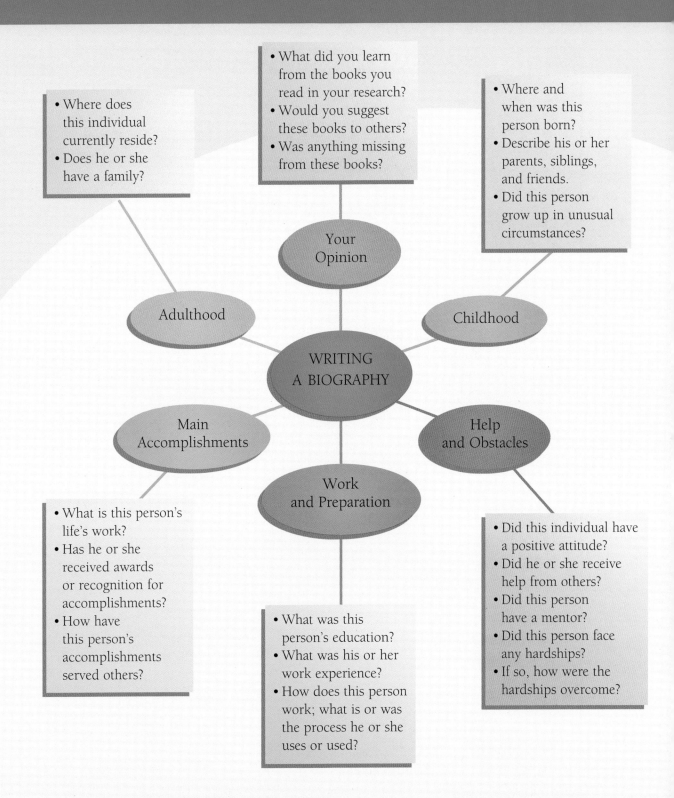

- Where does this individual currently reside?
- Does he or she have a family?

- What did you learn from the books you read in your research?
- Would you suggest these books to others?
- Was anything missing from these books?

- Where and when was this person born?
- Describe his or her parents, siblings, and friends.
- Did this person grow up in unusual circumstances?

Your Opinion

Adulthood

Childhood

WRITING A BIOGRAPHY

Main Accomplishments

Help and Obstacles

Work and Preparation

- What is this person's life's work?
- Has he or she received awards or recognition for accomplishments?
- How have this person's accomplishments served others?

- What was this person's education?
- What was his or her work experience?
- How does this person work; what is or was the process he or she uses or used?

- Did this individual have a positive attitude?
- Did he or she receive help from others?
- Did this person have a mentor?
- Did this person face any hardships?
- If so, how were the hardships overcome?

Timeline

YEAR	MARK ZUCKERBERG	WORLD EVENTS
1984	Mark Zuckerberg is born on May 14.	Apple Inc. releases the first Apple Macintosh computer.
2003	Mark Zuckerberg launches Facemash on October 28.	Apple Inc. launches the iTunes Music Store, an online store for downloading music.
2004	Mark Zuckerberg co-founds Facebook.	Tim Berners-Lee wins the first Millennium Technology Prize for inventing the World Wide Web.
2005	Facebook buys the domain name Facebook.com for $200,000.	News Corp buys social networking website Myspace on July 19.
2008	At age 23, Mark becomes the world's youngest self-made billionaire.	More than 1.5 billion people now use the internet.
2010	Mark is named *Time Magazine's* "Person of the Year."	*The Social Network*, a film about Mark Zuckerberg and the creation of Facebook, is released.
2012	Facebook becomes a **public company**.	Apple launches its iPhone 5.

Key Words

billionaire: a person possessing assets worth at least a billion dollars

doctorate: an advanced university degree

dormitory: a bedroom usually shared by several people at a university or other school

engineering: using science principles to manufacture, design, or construct something

entrepreneurs: people who create and take responsibility for a new company, invention, or idea

innovators: people who develop a new and often revolutionary way of thinking and doing something

marketing: the action of selling or promoting products or services

physics: the scientific study of matter and energy and how the two interact

principles: rules or standards

programs: sequences of coded instructions fed into a computer to make it complete specific tasks

psychology: the scientific study of the mind and its functions

public company: a company that sells shares on the stock market

reinvest: put the profit on a previous investment back into the same place

retailer: a business or person that sells goods directly to the consumer

search engine: a website that collects and organizes content from all over the internet

software developer: someone who creates the programs used to direct the operation of a computer

uploaded: put pictures, documents, video clips, etc. on a website

Index

Log on to www.av2books.com

AV² by Weigl brings you media enhanced books that support active learning. Go to www.av2books.com, and enter the special code found on page 2 of this book. You will gain access to enriched and enhanced content that supplements and complements this book. Content includes video, audio, web links, quizzes, a slide show, and activities.

Audio
Listen to sections of the book read aloud.

Video
Watch informative video clips.

Embedded Weblinks
Gain additional information for research.

Try This!
Complete activities and hands-on experiments.

WHAT'S ONLINE?

Try This!	Embedded Weblinks	Video	EXTRA FEATURES
Complete an activity about your childhood. Try this activity about key events. Complete an activity about overcoming obstacles. Write a biography. Try this timeline activity.	Find out more about Mark Zuckerberg's life. Learn more about Mark Zuckerberg's achievements. Check out this site about Mark Zuckerberg.	Watch a video about Mark Zuckerberg. Check out another video about Mark Zuckerberg.	**Audio** Listen to sections of the book read aloud. **Key Words** Study vocabulary, and complete a matching word activity. **Slide Show** View images and captions, and prepare a presentation. **Quizzes** Test your knowledge.

AV² was built to bridge the gap between print and digital. We encourage you to tell us what you like and what you want to see in the future.

Sign up to be an AV² Ambassador at www.av2books.com/ambassador.